PROFESSOR PHONICS GIVES SOUND ADVICE

Monica Foltzer, M. Ed.

Illustrated by
Jo-Ann Hoffmann, M. Ed.

Additional experimentation by
Rosemary Winkeljohann, M. Ed.

Third Printing   1968

Copyright, 1965
All rights reserved

ST. URSULA ACADEMY
1339 E. McMillan Street, Cincinnati, Ohio 45206

PREFACE

Phonics is a method of word recognition. It is not a method of reading although word recognition is its most fundamental technique.

The author's aim was to simplify the beginning work in phonetics by breaking it into smaller units than any she had known before. She felt that various areas could be organized and systematized more efficiently. Lastly, she wanted to present all the basic phonic elements needed within the covers of one book.

The author used the book with four groups of students - primary and remedial reading classes, foreign students and junior high students for articulation. Even though our language comprises 26 letters having about 42 sounds, there are phonetic rules which cover about 85% of the English language.

In English our five vowels cause the most trouble. The author teaches 16 basic vowel sounds which include 13 single vowel sounds and 3 double vowel sounds called diphthongs. These are easily divided into four groups.

The five short and five long vowel sounds make up the first two groups. The third group is the three single vowels which have a third sound. The last group of basic vowel sounds includes two plain diphthongs, oi and ou, and the murmur diphthong ur. Broken down into an easy division of 5, 5, 3, 3 the students can quite readily master the 16 basic vowel sounds.

Since the vast majority of all vowel sounds are the short sounds, the book treats of them first. When teaching a vowel, it is of great advantage to present all of its sounds at one time; for example, the short, the long and the third sound of a. All are memorized in that order but only the short sound of a developed.

It is important that ma, sa, etc., be blended together from the very beginning and not sounded in isolation. Flash cards are extremely helpful here as they focus attention on one combination of letters only.

Four indispensable procedures that will help teachers are: First, the use of memorized key words and rules. If key words are memorized, the students will always have a "home base" from which to start.

Secondly, written dictation is the only way a teacher can be sure the learner is hearing correctly. The facility of even first graders to "play by ear" and to guess is amazing.

Thirdly, what is taught must be applied the rest of the day in other classes. No word should be told if the student can sound it.

Fourthly, the beginning of the book is carefully organized. It is a step by step procedure. It is very important not to continue to the next page unless the previous pages are well grasped or phonetic indigestion will occur.

Phonics is not easy to teach the first few weeks so extra enthusiasm must be used. As soon as students realize they are being given the KEY to unlock new words, they are thrilled. Start on page 8.

Key words are the tools to unlock the sounds.
Memorize them well. Then –
    Think the key word;
    start the sound.

Key Words for the 16 Basic Vowel Sounds

1st sound or Short sound	2nd sound or Long sound	3rd sound	Diphthongs
apple	ate	all = a_3	owl = $\left.\begin{array}{l}\text{ou}\\\text{ow}\end{array}\right\}$
Eskimo	eat		
Indian	ice		oil = $\left.\begin{array}{l}\text{oi}\\\text{oy}\end{array}\right\}$
ostrich	old	to = o_3	
umbrella	use	put = u_3	urn = $\left.\begin{array}{l}\text{er}\\\text{ir}\\\text{ur}\end{array}\right\}$

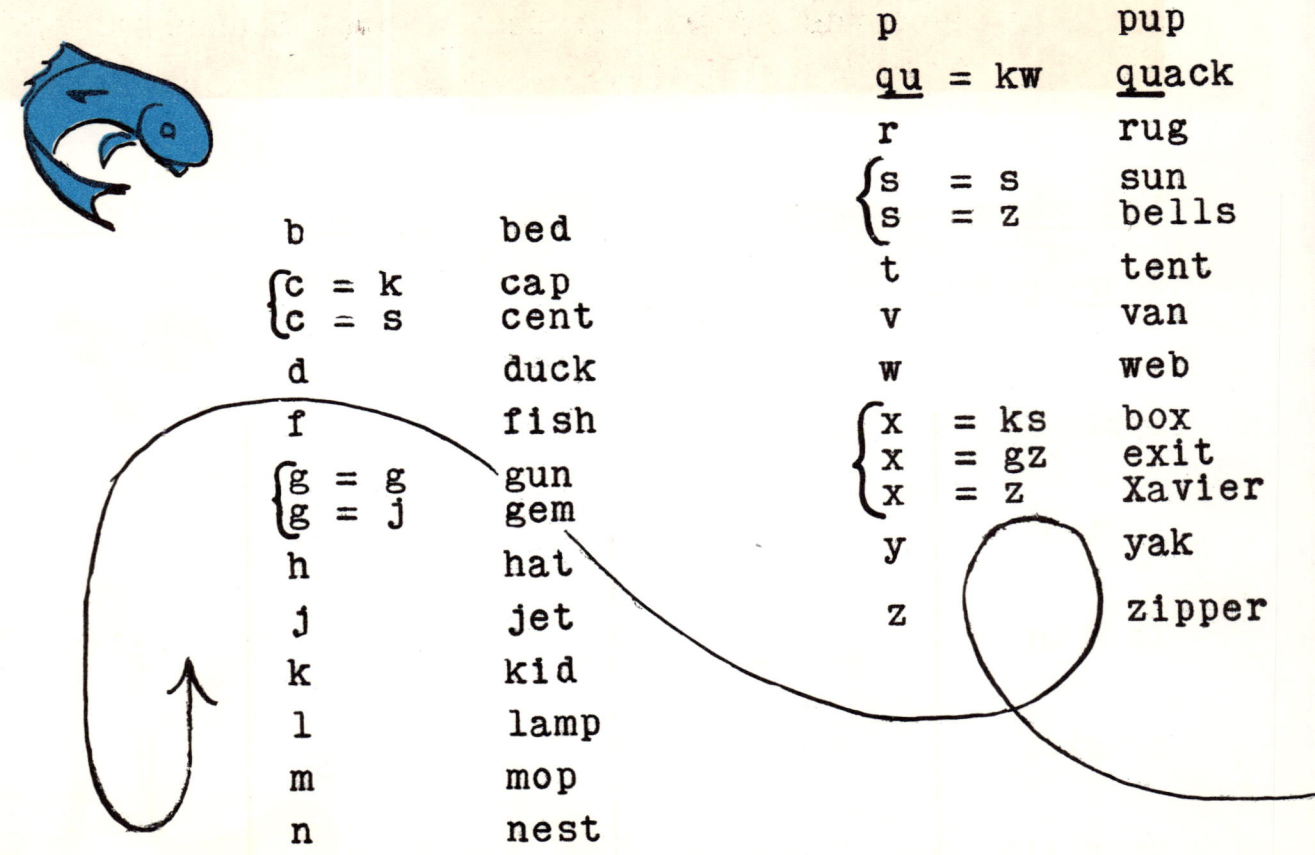

```
                                         p            pup
                                         qu = kw      quack
                                         r            rug
                                        ⎧s  = s       sun
                                        ⎩s  = z       bells
             b          bed              t            tent
            ⎧c = k      cap              v            van
            ⎩c = s      cent             w            web
             d          duck            ⎧x  = ks      box
             f          fish            ⎨x  = gz      exit
            ⎧g = g      gun             ⎩x  = z       Xavier
            ⎩g = j      gem              y            yak
             h          hat
             j          jet              z            zipper
             k          kid
             l          lamp
             m          mop
             n          nest
```

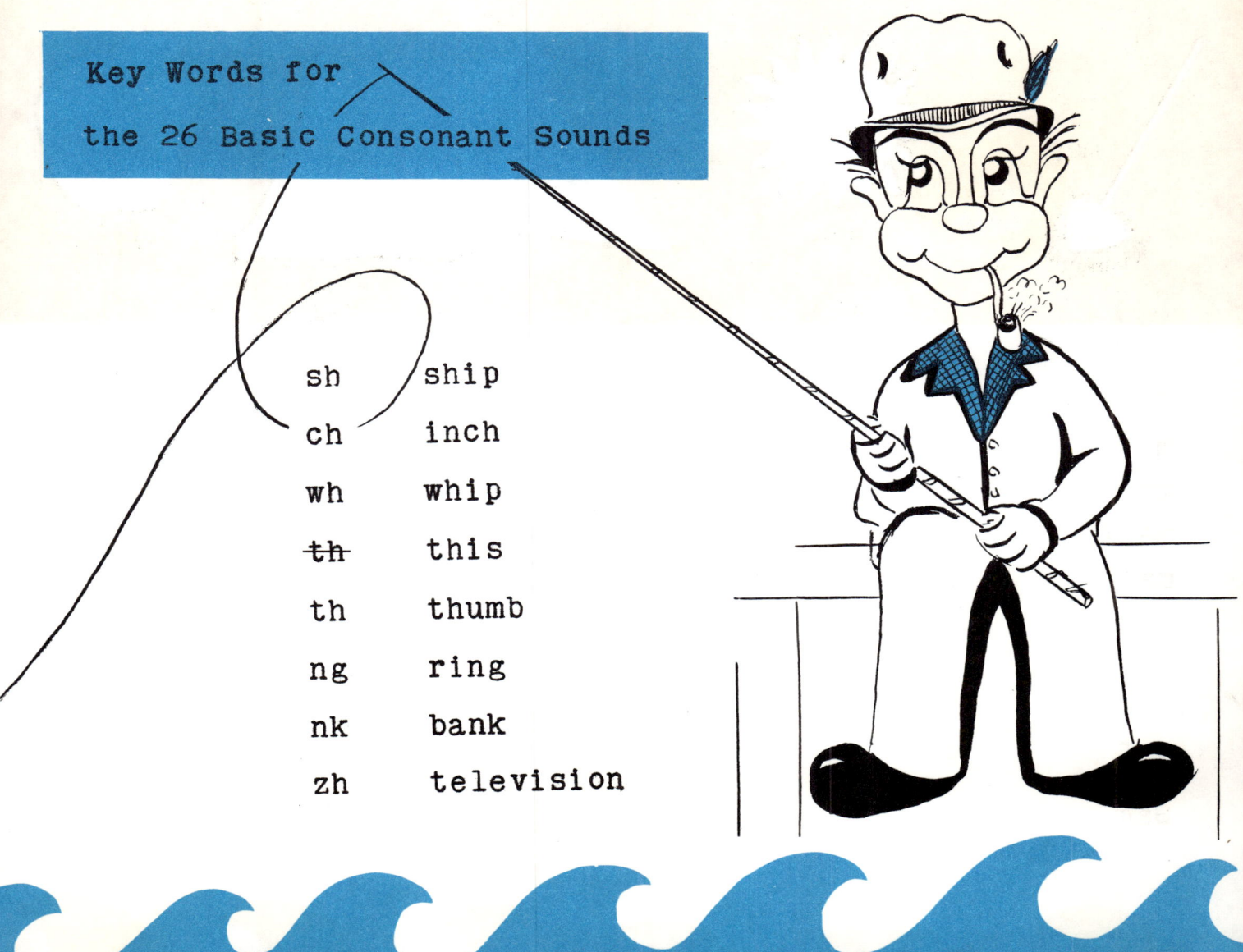

 mop
 sun
 tent
 apple

1	2	3	4	5	6
m	s	t	s	t	m
ma	sa	ta	sa	ta	ma
ma t	sa m	ta t	sa t	ta t	ma ss
mat	Sam	tat	sat	tat	mass

1	2	3	4	5	6
sat	mat	tat	tam	mass	at
Sam	am	mass	sat	sass	mat

1	2	3	4	5	6
d	g	d	g	t	s
da	ga	da	ga	ta	sa
da d	ga g	da m	ga s	ta g	sa d
dad	gag	dam	gas	tag	sad

1	2	3	4	5	6
am	dad	mad	at	add	tag
mat	sag	gas	sad	dam	dad
gag	ad	add	tag	mad	am

duck

gun

1	2	3	4	5	6
f	h	f	h	f	h
fa	ha	fa	ha	fa	ha
fa t	ha d	fa d	ha m	fa g	ha g
fat	had	fad	ham	fag	hag

1	2	3	4	5	6
mass	dam	sad	mad	sag	dad
gag	tag	am	sat	add	ham
at	fat	had	Tad	fad	hag

fish hat

1	2	3	4	5	6
r	p	r	p	r	p
ra	pa	ra	pa	ra	pa
ra t	pa d	ra g	pa t	ra p	pa m
rat	pad	rag	pat	rap	**Pam**

1	2	3	4	5	6
fag	fat	fad	Pam	sap	pat
ram	rag	rap	hag	rat	pap
had	gap	ham	map	tap	pad

1	2	3	4	5	6
n	b	n	b	n	b
na	ba	na	ba	na	ba
na p	ba t	na g	ba n	na b	ba d
nap	bat	nag	ban	nab	bad

1	2	3	4	5	6
and	nab	ban	fan	an	tab
Dan	ran	man	nap	gab	nag
dab	Nat	bad	bat	Ann	pan

nest bed

 cap
 kid
 lamp
 pack

1	2	3	4	5	6
c	l	c	l	k	ck
ca	la	ca	la	ka	ack
ca n	la p	ca p	la d	Ka t	la ck
can	lap	cap	lad	Kat	lack

1	2	3	4	5	6	7
cap	lap	lack	lad	rack	pat	pack
tack	cam	lag	back	cad	cab	gap
Kat	pal	can	rap	am	fad	man

1	2	3	4	5	6	7
v	j	w	qu	v	j	qu
va	ja	wa	qua	va	ja	qua
va n	ja b	wa g	qua ck	va t	ja m	qua ff
van	jab	wag	quack	vat	jam	quaff

1	2	3	4	5	6	7
quack	rag	van	rack	jab	nab	vat
bad	jack	fad	quaff	vat	wag	Jack
jam	had	dab	sap	gag	map	tab

1	2	3	4	5	6
y	z	y	l	y	t
ya	za	ya	la	ya	ta
ya p	za g	ya m	la x	ya k	ta x
yap	zag	yam	lax	yak	tax

1	2	3	4	5	6
zag	tax	wax	jam	yak	quaff
van	jag	yam	quack	jab	Jack
jack	Max	vat	lap	pal	lax

yak

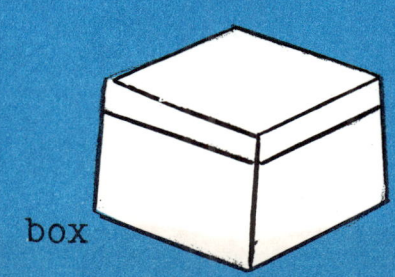
box

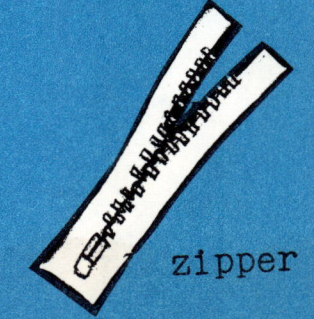
zipper

The short sound of a as in apple:

1	2	3	4	5	6	7
bad	dam	gap	lap	Nan	ram	tab
ban	Dan	had	lag	pat	ran	tax
bag	dab	hag	lack	pad	sat	van
bat	fan	ham	mat	pan	sag	vat
back	fad	hat	mad	pal	sad	wag
cap	fat	jab	man	quack	Sam	wax
can	gas	Jack	nap	rap	tag	yap
cab	gag	jam	nab	rag	tam	yam
dad	gab	lad	nag	rack	tan	yak

The short sound of i as in Indian:

1	2	3	4	5	6	7
bib	dim	him	kit	mid	rim	wick
big	dip	hid	kill	nick	rig	wig
bit	fin	hill	kiss	nip	rib	win
bill	fill	hip	lid	pin	sill	will
bin	fib	hit	lip	pick	sin	six
dig	fig	jig	lit	pill	sit	fix
did	fit	Jill	mitt	quick	tin	mix
dill	gig	Jim	mill	quiz	tip	Zip
din	gill	kid	miss	quill		fizz

Indian

Review of the short sounds of a and i:

1	2	3	4	5
cat	Liz	bid	pig	Nan
pass	pack	cad	miff	mass
kin	razz	gal	Pam	pick
tack	quit	rid	tiff	Tim
pip	kick	cam	Dick	rat
nick	lass	quip	map	tick
hat	Sis			
jazz	zip			
wit	hack			

umbrella

The short sound of <u>u</u> as in umbrella:

1	2	3	4	5	6	7
bug	cuff	fuzz	hub	muff	putt	sun
bud	cup	gum	huff	muck	pup	suck
but	cub	gun	jug	mug	run	tub
buff	dud	gut	jut	mum	rug	tug
buck	dull	gull	luck	nut	rub	tuck
bum	duck	hug	lug	nun	rum	**tut**
bus	dug	hut	lull	null	sub	tux
cud	fun	hull	mud	puff	sup	yum
cut	fuss	hum	muss	pug	sum	buzz

Review of the short sounds of a, i, and u:

1	2	3	4	5	6	7
jag	tat	dun	zip	cuff	jam	fill
cuss	Bud	rip	yap	quiz	dug	muss
pit	sick	Gus	fizz	lack	tax	gap
cull	mull	fag	tub	luck	but	mud
sap	tap	mutt	wax			
kid	rum	nib	will			
pun	sass	bun	hub			
sack	huff	sip	nap			
Jud	lick	dub	kill			

ostrich

The short sound of o as in ostrich:

1	2	3	4	5	6	7
bob	cop	fob	jog	mob	pox	sock
box	dot	got	job	mop	pop	sod
bog	doll	God	jot	mom	rot	sop
Bob	dock	gob	joss	mock	rob	tot
cot	dog	hot	lot	not	rod	top
cod	Don	hop	log	nod	rock	toss
cock	doff	hog	lock	pot	Rod	Tom
cob	fog	hod	loll	pock	Rob	tock
cog	fox	hock	lop	pod	sob	yon

Review of the short sounds of
<u>a</u>, <u>i</u>, <u>u</u>, and <u>o</u>:

1	2	3	4	5
loss	bit	<u>qu</u>ick	box	jam
tan	lob	toss	buzz	top
Jim	dad	wag	lag	pill
<u>qu</u>ack	fuss	hit	miss	tuck
fop	fib	jut	rob	nod
pug	boss	pin	vim	hug
nut	cab	pad	mock	job
lit	din	sum	hut	gum
mad	dull	yon	fix	rock

Eskimo

The short sound of e as in Eskimo:

1	2	3	4	5	6
bed	deck	keg	net	Rex	web
bell	fed	let	Ned	sell	wed
beg	fell	led	Nell	set	wen
bet	fen	leg	neck	tell	yes
Bess	get	less	pen	Ted	yell
Ben	hell	met	peg	ten	yen
beck	hen	men	pet	vex	yet
den	jet	Meg	peck	well	Zed
dell	jell	mess	red	wet	fez

Vowel Rule 1: When there is only one vowel in a word or syllable and the vowel comes between two consonants, the vowel is usually short.

1	2	3	4
bad	pep	back	fed
dill	vex	hep	Rob
sock	mat	dip	cup
hem	null	gun	fig
cut	dud	peg	nick
yell	set	lad	wed
web	bin	fell	rot
fog	well	tip	jell
did	Tom	less	yak

Review of the short sounds of all the vowels:

1	2	3	4	5	6	7
hum	bid	nip	yell	lass	fuzz	miff
win	mum	mess	dig	pet	dub	dot
cub	keg	van	pox	jag	jam	<u>qu</u>ick
yet	jazz	mob	will	<u>qu</u>it	pep	net
pick	sob	gas	buzz	sock	tag	rack
fad	lull	deck	lock	Zed	fop	<u>qu</u>iz
hot	yes	not	boss	led	mutt	moss
bus	den	rub	lax	loss	kin	bun
rag	cot	muff	sell	dog	less	sod

The short vowels with two consonants at the end:

1	2	3	4	5	6	7
pant	last	act	sand	dent	help	pelt
can't	past	land	bask	elm	jest	pest
fact	band	adz	task	elf	kept	quest
ramp	fast	pact	rasp	end	left	rend
hand	tact	mask	bend	fend	mend	rest
camp	ask	rapt	bent	felt	melt	rent
apt	lamp	ant	belt	hemp	next	self
damp	vamp	rant	best	held	nest	sent
vast	asp	mast	desk	helm	lent	send

Continued:  a b c

1	2	3	4	5	6	7
tend	yelp	hint	milk	its	punt	gulp
text	zest	jinx	risk	imp	lump	bump
test	disk	quilt	rift	loft	must	bulk
vend	fist	limp	silk	romp	pump	dust
vent	film	lift	sift	pomp	pulp	gust
wend	fits	lint	tilt	pond	tuft	hump
west	gilt	list	tint	lost	rust	hulk
welt	gift	zinc	wisp	fond	dump	just
wept	hilt	mist	wilt	cost	bust	jump

A **blend** is two or three consonants said together each keeping its own sound. These blends are used with the short sounds of the vowels.

1	2	3	4	5	6	7
bri m	cra b	drip	Fred	grid	prim	scruff
bre d	cra ck	drill	frog	grill	prig	scrub
bri g	cro p	drag	frost	grip	prop	scrap
bra g	cro ck	dram	grim	gruff	truck	sprig
bra d	cra m	drug	grub	prep	trot	strap
bra ss	dra b	from	grit	prod	trod	strip
bra n	cra g	frock	grin	prick	trap	stress
bra t	dre ss	frill	grab	press	trim	struck
cri b	dro p	fret	grand	pram	track	strut

More blends, continued:

1	2	3	4	5	6	7
twi t	clump	glad	plod	Scot	smug	squid
twi st	clan	glib	slot	scan	smut	stem
twi ll	click	glen	slop	scum	sniff	stud
twi n	clog	plus	sled	skull	snag	still
blo ck	flat	plan	slim	skin	snip	stab
bli ss	flax	plat	split	skim	snob	swam
blu ff	floss	plot	splint	skip	spell	swell
ble d	flex	plop	scat	smell	speck	swig
bla ck	glum	plug	scuff	smock	spat	swim

br   sc   st

A consonant <u>digraph</u> is two consonants which make one sound. The seven basic consonant digraphs below make seven new consonant sounds.

1 <u>ch</u>	2 <u>sh</u>	3 <u>wh</u>	4 <u>th</u>	5 <u>th</u>	6 <u>ng</u>	7 <u>nk</u>
chap	shell	when	this	thud	song	bank
chill	ship	which	them	think	hung	tank
chum	shut	whisk	that	thump	ring	blank
chess	shaft	whiz	then	theft	zing	blink
chest	sham	whip	with	thrash	clang	mink
chant	shed	whiff	than	thrill	slang	pink
rich	shun	whim	thus	path	swing	rink
inch	smash	whet		cloth	spring	honk
crunch	cash	whit		moth	string	sunk

After short vowels the sound of k is usually written ck.

1	2	3	4	5	6
back	crack	neck	brick	mock	duck
hack	track	peck	stick	rock	luck
jack	stack	check	thick	sock	muck
lack	smack	kick	prick	lock	suck
pack	snack	lick	trick	frock	tuck
quack	black	pick	chick	smock	struck
rack	slack	quick	click	block	chuck
sack	beck	wick	dock	clock	pluck
tack	deck	sick	cock	flock	truck

Vowel Rule 2: When there is only one vowel in a word or syllable and the vowel comes at the beginning of the word, the vowel is usually short.

1	2	3	4
add	egg	if	off
am	ebb	ill	odd
and	Ed	in	up
at	end	it	us
apt	elf	on	ups_e_t
an	elm	ox	u_nd_i_d

Short Vowel Key:

a_n elf i_s o_ften u_pside-down

After the voiceless t, p, k and f plurals, s is s.
After the voiced consonants in the plurals, the s has a z sound.

1	2	3	4	5	6
bats	cups	bluffs	rags	hams	wigs
kits	tots	lips	cabs	spells	suns
drips	sniffs	skips	drills	wins	logs
cots	fits	grips	pills	crams	sleds
clicks	gifts	nests	kings	yells	grins
tents	taps	traps	dogs	cans	nods
strips	trucks	cuts	tubs	kills	stabs
chests	sets	jets	twins	legs	drags
banks	specks	scraps	guns	swims	bugs

After short vowels the ch digraph is spelled tch.

1	2	3	4	5
batch	fetch	ditch	botch	Dutch
hatch	ketch	pitch	scotch	hutch
catch	retch	stitch	blotch	crutch
match	stretch	twitch	splotch	clutch
thatch	sketch	switch	notch	

There are five exceptions to this rule:

General review of the short sounds of the vowels:

1	2	3	4	5	6
brass	mend	drill	eggs	twist	prod
ranks	add	<u>q</u>uench	vest	witch	shift
kink	jilt	strung	bred	lost	glum
chant	fits	odd	jets	things	split
notch	fist	next	jest	whiz	spilt
up	crop	which	thus	wisp	ill
with	spell	ask	links	cloths	latch
zip	when	yell	bulk	cost	shed
vast	pluck	costs	them	clicks	desks

Many English words are made from two small words. They are compound words.

1	2	3	4
setup	dragnet	chestnut	mixup
kidnap	within	chopstick	gunshot
pumpkin	itself	blacktop	cobweb
pigskin	catnip	madman	brushoff
bandstand	hilltop	letup	backstop
deskpad	offhand	himself	tinsmith
shellfish	midship	zigzag	tiptop
cannot	sundeck	matchstick	clamshell
kickoff	bobcat	handgrip	padlock

Repeat the following after your teacher.   Can you see and hear the pattern?

1	2	3	4	5	6
us	use	bath	bathe	mop	mope
twin	twine	scrap	scrape	twin	twine
cub	cube	quit	quite	shin	shine
thin	thine	tack	take	sham	shame
led	lead	pad	paid	tub	tube
mitt	mite	whit	white	plan	plain
cloth	clothe	cut	cute	doll	dole
grip	gripe	snip	snipe	did	died
grim	grime	spit	spite	mutt	mute

When two vowels go awalking,
The first vowel does the talking.

Vowel Rule 3: When there are two vowels in a word or syllable, the first vowel is usually long and the second vowel is silent.

> When two vowels go awalking,
> The first vowel does the talking.

1	2	3	4	5	6	7
rake	boat	mete	cue	roar	maid	fume
made	fuse	joke	beat	lie	reach	cube
hue	suit	beet	yeast	goes	ripe	gay
gale	vase	tied	quail	wade	here	hear
way	fire	due	mane	hike	lime	door
low	wail	Pete	mine	dine	pile	mule
tore	each	daze	cope	cute	pure	same
died	soul	main	doze	coax	keep	bay
side	vine	pie	lute	use	mute	vane

Magic e words: The first vowel is long and the second vowel is silent.

1	2	3	4	5	6	7
ape	made	wave	mere	bike	rise	pipe
bale	nave	maze	eve	file	size	bite
cape	pane	rate	here	hide	time	wise
date	quake	vase	mete	wipe	vile	ripe
fake	raze	gave	eke	kite	wife	mile
game	safe	name	Pete	like	quite	pine
hate	tame	care	Eve	mine	dine	quire
jade	vale	Dave	ire	nine	dire	five
lame	wade	save	dime	pile	wine	side

41

Magic e words, continued:

1	2	3	4	5	6	7
lake	Dave	joke	vote	hope	cube	stove
tale	fire	lobe	woke	pole	cute	dude
rake	fine	mole	wore	pore	duke	sole
nape	hire	note	yoke	rose	fume	lure
sale	site	poke	zone	rode	Luke	pure
pare	vine	quote	code	robe	mute	tube
lame	bone	rove	dole	tore	cure	mule
take	cope	sore	dome	wove	cone	tune
care	doze	tone	hole	home	dote	dune

A **vowel** **digraph** contains two vowels which make one sound. In these **regular** vowel digraphs the first vowel is long, the second vowel is silent.

1	2	3	4	5	6	7
aim	pain	day	week	loaf	tow	doe
bail	quail	way	deep	moan	bow	sue
fair	raid	say	jeer	door	sow	cue
gain	sail	bee	oak	soak	hoed	hue
hail	vain	feed	boat	road	foe	suit
jail	tail	keep	coal	coat	goes	hoax
lain	wait	queer	coax	floor	Joe	sued
maid	ray	need	foam	low	toes	Sue
nail	may	seek	goal	row	flow	due

The basic consonant digraphs with long vowels:

1 sh	2 ch	3 wh	4 ~~th~~ (voiced)	5 th (voiceless)
shame	chair	while	these	three
sheep	chase	wheat	those	thrive
show	cheat	white	thine	throat
shade	chose	whine	blithe	throne
shine	chain	whale	bathe	throw
share	each	wheel	clothe	growth
sheet	speech	wheeze	lathe	faith
shone	peach	whoa	tithe	teeth
shake	reach		lithe	oath

ch wh th sh

After short vowels, the sound of k is written ck; after long vowels the sound of k is written k.

1	2	3	4	5	6
back	bake	lack	lake	sock	soak
Jack	Jake	chock	choke	black	Blake
tack	take	peck	peek	cock	coke
stock	stoke	check	cheek	smock	smoke
quack	quake	Dick	dike	clock	cloak
rack	rake	lick	like	duck	duke
sack	sake	pick	pike	shack	shake
slack	slake	crock	croak	stack	stake

Vowel Rule 4: When there is only one vowel in a word or syllable and the vowel comes at the end, the vowel is usually long.

1	2	3	4	5	6	7
be	so	he	spy	no	thy	ye
dry	by	why	hi	fry	she	sky
me	cry	we	go	shy	my	fly

Sentences using long vowels:

1. We came to bake a cake.
2. Did he see the white duck?
3. I paid a dime for the kite.
4. He got in the hole.
5. The dog likes the bones.
6. The fire is on this side.
7. He has tears on his cheeks.
8. Pete has a fine time here.
9. She is to keep the pup.
10. Joe goes here to wade.
11. The gray twig will float.
12. The red cloak was clean.

REVIEW: Give the number of the rule and say the rule.

1 at	11 jot	21 ray	31 here	41 an	51 cry
2 joke	12 wick	22 goes	32 soar	42 day	52 low
3 fuse	13 he	23 mute	33 keep	43 wipe	53 each
4 fox	14 ox	24 end	34 elm	44 so	54 zip
5 suit	15 gum	25 den	35 we	45 neat	55 sore
6 by	16 am	26 ill	36 odd	46 fill	56 sin
7 cut	17 no	27 me	37 us	47 elf	57 lied
8 vim	18 cue	28 my	38 hop	48 be	58 yes
9 ebb	19 lake	29 back	39 go	49 fly	59 pill
10 soul	20 yeast	30 coax	40 due	50 goal	60 up

Blends with the long sound of the vowels:

1	2	3	4	5	6	7
brake	drain	grown	tribe	screech	throw	bleak
bride	drive	grape	trite	shrine	throat	blade
brave	dream	grade	tree	sprite	three	blow
brain	drone	groan	treat	sprain	throne	blaze
Crete	dried	gray	tray	spray	thrive	bleed
crate	frame	probe	train	strike	twain	cloak
cream	froze	prose	screen	strife	tweed	clean
crane	fried	prize	scream	stroke	tweak	claim
creep	green	pray	scrape	strode	twine	close

dr sc tw cl st

Blends with the long sound of the vowels, continued:

1	2	3	4	5	6
floor	plead	scream	speak	state	breeze
flare	play	smile	spied	stay	crease
float	slope	smear	speed	stream	freeze
flame	slave	smoke	squeak	stripe	praise
glow	sleet	snow	squeal	steal	sneeze
glaze	slay	snake	square	sweep	sleeve
gleam	scale	snore	stole	sway	breathe
plain	score	sneer	stain	sweet	please
pleat	skate	spoke	stake	swipe	squeeze

gl

br

Consonant digraphs reviewing long and short vowels:

1	2	3	4	5	6	7
<u>sh</u>	<u>ch</u>	<s><u>th</u></s>	<u>wh</u>	<u>th</u>	<u>ng</u>	<u>nk</u>
shot	chat	this	when	thin	sang	sank
shall	cheap	those	which	thank	rang	sink
shame	choke	these	whiz	thick	sung	bunk
sheep	much	than	while	thing	king	junk
rash	such	clothe	why	three	wing	rank
shelf	chin	thus	white	path	long	link
crush	beach	loathe	whisk	fourth	bring	tank
crash	flinch	breathe	wheel	cloth	sting	think

Vowel Rule 5: When a is followed by u, w, r, ll and lt in the same syllable, it often has the third sound of a, the Italian ä.

1	2	3	4	5	6
haul	raw	car	call	salt	pause
Paul	flaw	farm	small	halt	squall
fault	dawn	yarn	ball	Walt	hard

---

fraud	yaw	lawn	gauze	drawl	taunt
yawn	starch	part	crawl	jaunt	scrawl
shark	jaw	launch	saw	scar	Maud
daunt	start	bark	malt	clause	hall
law	pawn	drawn	stall	wall	garb
vault	cause	lark	sharp	haunt	fall

au   aw   alt

The words containing the third sound of o̅ and u̅ are really non-phonetic words. Webster's dictionaries use the long and short oo for their phonetic spelling while the Thorndike and similar dictionaries use the two dot and one dot u. Since much confusion results because school text glossaries use one or the other, teaching these sounds originally as the third sound of o̅ and u̅ gives one a practical bridge to link the two types of diacritical marks.

The third sound of a, o, and u:

1	2	3	4
claw	do	put	y̸our
taunt	to	push	sho̸u̸ld
draw	lose	pull	b<u>u</u>ll<u>e</u>t
mall	move	bush	b<u>u</u>sh<u>e</u>l
shark	w̸ho	puss	p<u>u</u>sh<u>i</u>ng
sprawl	shoe	b<u>u</u>ll<u>y</u>	p<u>u</u>lp<u>i</u>t
hawk	tw̸o	full	p<u>u</u>ll<u>e</u>t
straw	w̸hom	bull	b<u>u</u>llfr<u>o</u>g
yard	tomb̸	wo̸u̸ld	p<u>u</u>dd<u>i</u>ng

Which word has the short, the long or the third sound of a?

1 and	11 rain	21 wall	31 wade	41 haul	51 bad
2 call	12 am	22 fault	32 pain	42 game	52 dawn
3 bail	13 Paul	23 nap	33 ball	43 vault	53 pack
4 wax	14 sag	24 lane	34 Jap	44 jail	54 date
5 flaw	15 halt	25 fraud	35 small	45 gag	55 cause
6 an	16 nape	26 pat	36 rack	46 safe	56 zag
7 hate	17 tab	27 saw	37 made	47 fan	57 tall
8 lawn	18 salt	28 vase	38 maid	48 Maud	58 dam
9 cave	19 yam	29 mad	39 law	49 cab	59 pawn
10 van	20 fake	30 raw	40 lax	50 yawn	60 daze

Diphthong: two vowels in one syllable making one double vowel sound.
We have four plain diphthongs: oi, oy, ou, ow.

1	2	3	4	5	6	7
how	oil	drown	sound	fowl	spout	joint
cow	boil	coin	hoist	coy	noise	cloud
bow	toil	sow	mouse	down	mount	cowl
now	soil	point	quoit	soy	moist	spoil
out	join	foil	round	void	gown	found
our	boy	house	vow	count	broil	brown
sour	joy	coil	poise	town	prowl	joist
pout	Roy	owl	pound	foist	mouth	plow
shout	toy	oink	howl	clown	crown	south

owl

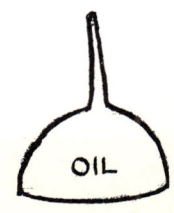
oil

The <u>murmur</u> diphthongs are <u>ar</u>, <u>or</u>, <u>er</u>, <u>ir</u>, <u>ur</u>. An <u>r</u> is often called a half-vowel. It changes the sound of the preceding vowel.

1	2	3	4	5	6	7
bar	or	her	dart	sort	snort	stern
arm	for	fern	pert	term	q<u>u</u>irk	fir
jar	nor	perk	sir	ark	harm	storm
harp	born	bird	sport	skirt	blurt	surf
spark	cord	dirt	curl	York	smart	twirl
char	fork	firm	barn	clerk	jerk	form
Carl	lord	burn	torn	stir	nurse	hurt
mark	morn	curb	nerve	horn	corn	hark
lard	pork	fur	purr	card	hark	

ar   or   ur   er   ir

urn

GENERAL REVIEW

1	2	3	4	5	6
slam	who	thank	swarm	plow	spurn
sound	stern	could	pull	slow	which
plied	with	spite	churn	bleat	owl
short	clerk	point	string	dwarf	grow
awl	squawk	daub	tomb	noise	stir
grape	chip	such	warmth	full	would
clown	push	ground	should	think	squint
snow	sour	gleam	ponds	spun	harm
put	shark	burnt	why	loud	crush

Vowel Rule 6: When y comes at the end of a two or more syllable word, y has the sound of long e if the y syllable is unaccented.

Vowel Rule 6:

1	2	3	4	5	6
funny	penny	sloppy	baby	soapy	pony
ugly	bunny	puppy	wavy	smoky	shady
happy	poppy	lefty	tidy	lady	flaky

> Vowel Rule 7: When y comes at the end of a two or more syllable word, y has the sound of long i if the y syllable is accented.

1	2	3	4	5
reply	defy	edify	ratify	dignify
supply	comply	magnify	signify	electrify
apply	ally	multiply	occupy	identify

The suffix ed has three sounds.
   After t and d it says ĕd forming a new syllable.
   It says t after s, x, k, ck, sh, ch, p and f.
   After every other sound it says d.

ed = ĕd		ed = t		ed = d	
tinted	rested	mapped	pecked	fanned	planned
listed	sifted	mixed	huffed	sobbed	mobbed
blended	nested	licked	stressed	flagged	dinned
drifted	rented	snapped	puffed	dammed	trilled
rusted	blotted	inched	stripped	scrubbed	hugged
ended	hinted	topped	slashed	bobbed	manned
misted	rotted	trapped	dressed	tilled	stilled
planted	wended	dropped	slapped	tugged	robbed

ed   *ed* *ed*

Vowel Rule 8: When words end with the suffix ing, ed or er, the first vowel is usually short if it comes before two consonants.

1	2	3	4	5
bedding	stopper	rubbed	bending	jumper
dipping	shutter	rammed	tramping	printer
jotting	drummer	skinned	planting	helper
fretting	robber	yelled	fishing	vender
getting	sitter	hemmed	snatching	softer
tossing	runner	canned	costing	tilted
jigging	swimmer	pinned	lisping	jested
trapping	flatter	dragged	bumping	landed
splitting	redder	dulled	clicking	quilted

ing   *ed*   *er*

> Vowel Rule 9: When words end with the suffix ing, ed or er, the first vowel is usually long if it comes before a single consonant.

1	2	3	4	5
hating	grading	wider	tamer	noted
taming	probing	filer	biter	shaded
riding	thriving	wader	wiser	sided
sliding	stating	hiker	voter	craned
fuming	smiling	miner	user	cubed
zoning	flaming	cuter	scraper	dared
voting	sloping	riper	blazer	liked
shaking	stroking	joker	skater	skated
naming	swiping	safer	smoker	choked

Which sound does the ed say? d, ed, or t?

1	2	3	4	5	6
liked	reached	lasted	picked	coasted	sloped
voted	pined	mopped	buzzed	baked	noted
called	robbed	boxed	waded	bleached	messed
smoked	printed	sailed	wailed	plotted	pointed
tested	shaded	played	cubed	perched	fixed
wheeled	turned	slammed			
heated	kicked	twisted			
bragged	penned	dreamed			
cashed	dusted	boiled			
willed	splashed	filled			
beaded	mended	lifted			
stopped	braided	cuffed			

Review of Vowel Rules 6, 7, 8, 9

1	2	3	4	5
shaky	sandy	matching	Davy	supply
tending	sender	dripped	stroking	scored
getting	thinking	reply	risking	bony
rented	slider	smoker	poked	flinging
rider	kitty	betting	swelter	occupy
ridding	twisted	gilted	drifted	throbbed
zipper	gliding	mixed	packed	scared
wishing	stocking	adding	skater	sloping
navy	snubbed	crated	satisfy	slopping

a e i o u

bells

Most consonants have one sound only; however, c, x and q have no sounds of their own.

The consonants c, x, g and s have more than one sound. There is a hard and soft c and g, three sounds for x and two sounds for s. We have rules to help us with these.

Consonant s Rules: se at the end of a word often has the sound of z.

nose   rise   hose   wise   those   please

s after voiced consonants says z.

cars   rugs   bells   fans   rods   bibs

c   qu   x

Consonant c Rules: Hard c - c says k before a, o, u.

1	2	3	4	5	6
case	cove	cuff	coin	cue	cord
coat	cob	cube	count	cast	cur

Soft c - c says s before e, i, y.

1	2	3	4	5	6	7
cent	cede	cease	cyst	ice	glance	lance
cell	Celt	cite	cinch	thence	bounce	fence
dice	place	hence	trace	dance	mince	nice

c before consonants says k.

clown   cross   cycle   creed   claim

cent

Hard and soft c mixed

1	2	3	4	5	6
dunce	cord	France	coast	cedar	circle
since	face	curve	can't	carpet	princess
code	thrice	corpse	center	circus	cynic
twice	coal	cause	civic	citrus	cistern
curt	grace	curb	cellar	Cyprus	pencil
coach	cash	cork	cinder	cypress	cider
cave	cull	curse	censor	cycle	Cyclops
coil	space	prince	census	cyclone	bicycle
coax	cove	trance	chance	civil	accept

Consonant g Rules: Hard g - g says g before a, o, u.

1	2	3	4	5	6
game	goat	gulp	gash	gulch	gale
gaze	gong	gush	goad	gave	gay

Soft g - ge says j at the end of a word.

1	2	3	4	5	6
age	sledge	urge	cringe	judge	wage
huge	lodge	gorge	splurge	badge	large

At the beginning of a word ge, gi, gy may be hard or soft g.

1	2	3	4	5	6
gem	gibe	gist	gift	get	gig
germ	gym	gin	girl	gird	gild

Hard and soft g - mixed

1	2	3	4	5	6
goes	serge	singe	page	tragic	gentle
gene	goal	gage	gill	German	suggest
merge	wedge	charge	bridge	goblin	gypsum
ridge	gauze	edge	girth	magic	giant
gosh	fudge	grudge	smudge	gender	angel
plunge	gulf	gear	gee	garden	garment
gorge	gel	hinge	trudge	giblet	gutter
twinge	fringe	gust	gape	ginger	gerund
gang	gall	dodge	hedge	gizzard	gunner

gem

Some vowel combinations form both regular and irregular digraphs. The regular vowel digraphs always have the first vowel long and the second silent. The irregular vowel digraphs can have any other of the basic vowel sounds.

By placing them on a page together one can distinguish them more easily. The most difficult of all is the ou combination which is also a diphthong.

The regular vowel digraph ie says the long sound of i.

1	2	3	4	5	6	7
die	lie	ties	fie	cried	flies	tried
tie	died	vie	cries	fries	dried	tries
pie	lied	vied	skies	fried	dries	rye

The irregular vowel digraph ie says the long sound of e.

1	2	3	4	5	6
field	yield	brief	chief	shield	belief
fiend	piece	grief	thief	priest	believe
wield	niece	grieves	thieves	shriek	relief

The regular vowel digraph oo says long o in two words - **door** and **floor.**

> The irregular vowel digraph oo says the third sound of u.

1	2	3	4	5	6
book	good	took	crook	stood	books
cook	hook	wood	brook	nook	cooks
foot	look	wool	shook	hood	poor

Another irregular vowel digraph oo says the third sound of o.

1	2	3	4	5	6	7
food	fool	ooze	moon	boom	pool	spoon
soon	room	root	loop	noon	zoom	shoot
cool	boot	roof	coop	tool	hoop	loose

 Regular Digraph   Irregular Digraphs

ē̄a̸		ĕa̸	ø̸ā	ear=ŭr	ear=är
eat	read	read	break	earn	heart
heat	lead	lead	great	earth	hearty
beat	tear	tear	steak	early	hearten
leaf	each	wealth		earnest	hearth
sea	beach	dead		heard	hearken
east	cheat	bread		learn	heartfelt
dear	clean	steady		pearl	heartsick
least	plead	heavy		search	heartless
bead	gleam	dread		yearn	heartbeat

Review of regular and irregular vowel digraphs: **ea** **oo** **ie**

1	2	3	4	5	6	7
eat	dealt	hook	yeast	wool	means	ready
heaven	foot	beat	stood	noon	wood	room
spoon	leaf	shoot	fried	steak	least	heart
fool	weather	dread	bead	brief	skies	field
lean	loop	boot	meal	fear	heat	meant
brook	break	died	food	soon	shield	cool
leather	piece	took	great	spread	crook	seal
loose	good	dean	thief	poor	chief	flies
dear	east	earn	shook	heard	dead	feather

Long sound of u: *u*

Regular Digraph		Irregular Digraph			Magic e	
cue	sue	few	feud	news	cube	fuse
hue	suit	new	mew	deuce	fume	mule
due	dues	pew	dew	hew	mute	cure

Exceptions to long u: after r, j, ch, and l blend u has the third sound of o.

rude	threw	Jew	chew	flew	crew
rule	drew	jute	blue	plume	flue
true	Jude	Judy	blew	flute	crude
rue	Jupiter	jubilee	clue	brute	glue

Regular Digraph		Irregular Digraph	
ēi̸		ei = ā	eig̸h = ā
either	deceit	veil	eight
neither	deceive	rein	weigh
seize	conceit	skein	sleigh
ceiling	perceive	feig̸n	neighbor
leisure	receive	vein	eighty
seizure	receiver	ҟeir	eighth
weird	receip̸t	their	freight
key	weir	they	weight
monkey	conceive	obey	neighborly

ei

Besides the diphthong ou sound, ou has at least six digraph sounds:

Regular Digraph   Irregular Digraphs

ō	ŏ	ŭ	o₃	u₃	our = ur
soul	cough	double	soup	could	courage
though	trough	trouble	group	would	flourish
dough	ought	touch	you	should	nourish
court	thought	country	youth	your	scourge
mourn	brought	young	wound	yours	courtesy
course	sought	southern	through		courteous
pour	fought	couple	tour		journey
four	bought	famous	tourist		journal

77

HELPFUL VOWEL-SOUND COMPARISONS

Digraph	Diphthong	Long	Short	Long	Short
1	2	3	4	5	6
shown	brow	raged	edge	able	fumble
follow	frown	cage	nudge	trifle	sprinkle
shadow	prow	page	pledge	noble	mantle
flow	browse	stage	budge	cable	uncle
mow	powder	huge	sledge	rifle	struggle
bow	bow	sage	drudge	fable	sniffle
sow	sow	gaged	ledge	maple	brittle
row	row	oblige	lodge	stable	trample

GENERAL REVIEW

1	2	3	4	5	6
thicker	hoping	flocking	key	could	trance
young	hopping	loose	cool	whiter	flaunt
fling	wended	court	spurn	neighbor	slink
twice	sq̲u̲elch	heart	wealth	brook	nourish
chew	neither	spruce	flashing	thief	smudge
hood	yield	cried	threw	cease	richer
snappy	later	wound	sq̲u̲ish	shaming	germ
longing	latter	veil	bought	coach	twinge
braided	couch	drawl	search	clue	gem

x *y* *z*

Part II

Minor Rules

Exceptions

Reference Pages

Sound the vowel in the unaccented syllable like short — short u as in circus. This is the schwa and is written as an inverted e in dictionaries.

a	a	e	i	o	u
along	bridal	bitten	muffin	beckon	rumpus
away	local	stiffen	cabin	Boston	circus
ago	floral	sudden	bobbin	bottom	locust
alike	normal	towel	robin	cannon	crocus
amuse	mortal	kennel	victim	kingdom	humus
awake	lizard	camel	pencil	lemon	lawful
ajar	cadet	burden	pupil	carbon	sinful
alone	canal	vessel	stupid	fathom	willful
affirm	caress	pocket	denim	parrot	fitful

A prefix is a syllable placed before a root word to change the meaning.

1	2	3	4	5
inside	display	prepaid	rejoin	consult
inflate	distrust	prevent	return	confess
invite	discuss	prefer	retrace	construct
entire	impress	misstep	excel	protect
enjoy	impart	mistake	exceed	provide
enroll	implore	mistrust	expect	propel
unfit	declare	perhaps	admit	combine
unknown	define	perform	admire	complain
undo	defrost	perspire	advice	command

in

de

con

A suffix is an ending or a syllable placed after a root word to change the meaning.

1	2	3	4	5
careful	useless	selfish	guidance	action
joyful	cloudless	boyish	distance	notion
cheerful	harmless	foolish	nuisance	station
loudly	statement	upward	joyous	pleasant
nearly	treatment	forward	nervous	remnant
weekly	pavement	westward	famous	merchant
strongest	darkness	likewise	dental	suitable
highest	sadness	sidewise	formal	capable
smoothest	plainness	lengthwise	central	breakable

less   tion

Silent letters - these are also consonant digraphs:

1 w̸r	2 k̸n	3 g̸n	4 mb̸	5 mn̸
wrap	know	gnat	lamb	hymn
write	knee	gnash	dumb	damn
wrote	knife	gnome	bomb	limn
wrong	knew	gnaw	limb	damned
wrench	knit	gnarl	crumb	column
wring	knob	sign	climb	autumn
wrist	knock	assign	comb	solemn
wreck	knelt	design	thumb	condemn
wren	knot	consign	numb	contemn

silent l	silent h	silent u	silent e	silent t
1	2	3	4	5
folk	hour	guess	ample	often
calf	school	guy	simple	listen
half	honest	guard	sample	fasten
halves	ghost	guest	little	soften
calm	John	guide	puzzle	whistle
palm	Thomas	guilt	tremble	castle
alms	ghastly	built	twinkle	bristle
chalk	heir	buy	sizzle	hustle
walk	honor	buoy	scramble	nestle

Almost every exception to the murmur diphthongs has the short vowel sound.

1	2	3	4
carry	berry	mirror	sorry
Harry	merry	cirrus	sorrow
marry	merit	syrup	morrow
marrow	very	irregular	orange
Larry	Jerry	irritate	Florida
carrot	ferry	irritant	forest
narrow	perish	irrigate	forage
tarry	cherry	irresolute	horrid
Carol	derrick	stirrup	torrid

In some words when two vowels appear together, they are each sounded separately. They are, therefore, not vowel digraphs.

1	2	3	4	5	6
di al	doer	trio	trial	studio	aviator
re al	Joey	Noel	rodeo	truant	science
are a	neon	Suez	quiet	period	patriot
bi as	Iowa	Ohio	radio	violin	theater
gi ant	liar	client	fluid	medium	violet
di et	ruin	fiery	oasis	liable	reliant
bo a	Noah	react	piano	heroic	manual
du al	poet	fluent	Maria	theory	variety
di ary	lion	plier	piety	orient	nucleus

All of these words are non-phonetic. They are long instead of short.

old 1	olt 2	oll 3	ost 4	ind 5	ild 6
cold	bolt	boll	most	find	mild
fold	colt	roll	post	hind	wild
gold	dolt	toll	host	kind	child
hold	jolt	stroll	ghost	mind	wilder
sold	molt	scroll	ghostly	rind	milder
told	volt	tolling	posting	wind	mildest
scold	bolts	roller	poster	blind	wildest
colds	molts	rolls	hostess	grind	mildly

old   olt ind   ost

Non-phonetic words in which every <u>o</u> is a short <u>u</u>:

1	2	3	4	5	6
ton	dove	come	mother	money	comfort
son	love	comely	brother	month	company
won	lovely	color	smother	Monday	compass
of	shove	honey	covering	lover	comforter
front	glove	coming	covenant	loving	nothing
wonder	cover	covet	covetous	monk	slovenly
none	govern	stomach	governor	dozen	tongue
some	above	covert	hover	oven	monkey
done	London	other	lovable	become	wondrous

COMMON WORDS WHICH ARE NOT PHONETIC

1	2	3	4	5	6	7
are	child	friend	laugh	shoe	truth	women
any	could	give	lose	some	twelve	work
again	come	gone	many	sure	view	who
answer	does	have	one	should	very	watch
been	done	heard	once	sugar	was	where
busy	don't	his	pretty	two	want	world
blood	eye	iron	sew	there	were	would
beauty	flood	island	said	toward	woman	you
color	find	love	says	their	wash	your
bury	height	juice	junior	genius	senior	onion

Special Consonant Digraphs: gh has three variations:

ph = f	gh = f	gh = g	silent gh
1	2	3	4
phone	laugh	ghost	high
phonics	laughter	ghostly	sigh
elephant	laughing	aghast	thigh
phrase	tough	ghastly	light
Philip	rough	ghoul	bright
orphan	roughly	ghetto	slight
alphabet	enough	Ghent	fright
prophet	cough	Ghana	might
paragraph	trough	gherkin	straight

ch has three sounds: ch has two spellings:

ch	ch = sh	ch = k		ch	tu = ch
	(French)	(Greek)			
check	chagrin	scheme		cheese	nature
chatter	Chevrolet	ache		chapter	moisture
chubby	chute	Christmas		children	creature
crutch	parachute	echo		change	future
inch	chauffeur	chemist		pitcher	lecture
scratch	charade	character		kitchen	structure
stretch	chevron	mechanic		speech	picture
sketch	chaperon	stomach		teacher	posture
merchant	Chicago	chrome		branch	actual

The sh sound has five different spellings besides sh.

tion = shun	sion = shun	ci / ti = sh	su = sh	ch = sh
nation	mission	facial	sure	chiffon
station	fission	racial	assure	Charlotte
vacation	pension	glacier	reassure	chic
position	tension	spacious	fissure	chalet
protection	session	special	insure	chateau
quotation	confession	precious	censure	crochet
attention	extension	partial	pressure	chamois
condition	mansion	patient	erasure	machine
observation	compassion	initial	sugar	chef

x has three sounds:

One consonant sound has no distinctive spelling.

ks	gz	z	
lax	exit	Xavier	Asia
mix	exam	xenon	fusion
hex	exist	xanthin	vision
tax	exult	xȳlem	television
Rex	exact	xȳloid	glazier
fix	exalt	xȳlene	usual
fox	example		measure
wax	exhaust		azure
box	exhibit		seizure

$\left.\begin{array}{l}\text{si, zi}\\\text{su, zu}\end{array}\right\} = $ zh

CONSONANT RULES IN PHONICS

I. Rules for the sound of the letter c

    1. Hard c - c says k before a, o, u
    2. Soft c - c says s before e, i, y
    3. Before a consonant c says k

II. Rules for the sound of the letter g

    1. Hard g - g says g before a, o, u
    2. Soft g - ge says j at the end of a word
    3. At the beginning of a word, ge, gi, gy may be hard or soft g

III. Rules for the sound of the letter s

    1. At the end of a word, se often has the sound of z
    2. After voiced consonants s says z

IV. Rules for the sound of the letter x

    1. At the end of a word, x says ks
    2. At the end of the syllable ex, x may say gz or ks
    3. At the beginning of a word, x says z

KEEP IN TRIM

PRACTICE THE VOWEL RULES

VOWEL RULES

1. When there is only one vowel in a word or syllable and the vowel comes between two consonants, the vowel is usually short.

2. When there is only one vowel in a word or syllable and the vowel comes at the beginning of the word, the vowel is usually short.

3. When there are two vowels in a word or syllable, the first vowel is usually long and the second is silent.

VOWEL RULES, CONTINUED

4. When there is only one vowel in a word or syllable and the vowel comes at the end, the vowel is usually long.

5. When <u>a</u> is followed by <u>u</u>, <u>w</u>, <u>r</u>, <u>ll</u>, and <u>lt</u> in the same syllable, it often has the third sound of <u>a</u>, the Italian <u>ä</u>.

6. When <u>y</u> comes at the end of a two or more syllable word, <u>y</u> has the sound of long <u>e</u> if the <u>y</u> syllable is unaccented.

7. When <u>y</u> comes at the end of a two or more syllable word, <u>y</u> has the sound of long <u>i</u> if the <u>y</u> syllable is accented.

8. When words end with the suffix <u>ing</u>, <u>ed</u> or <u>er</u>, the first vowel is usually short if it comes before two consonants.

9. When words end with the suffix <u>ing</u>, <u>ed</u> or <u>er</u>, the first vowel is usually long if it comes before a single consonant.

RULES FOR SYLLABICATION

1. A word containing one vowel <u>sound</u> is never divided.

    fat   fact   fame   curl

2. A compound word is divided between the two simple words.

    up-set   in-to   sun-beam   bath-room

3. If a word has a prefix, it is divided between the prefix and the root.

    mis-take   un-loose   ex-cel   ad-mit

4. If a word has a suffix, it is divided between the root and the suffix.

    plant-ed   end-ed   sing-ing   high-ness

<u>Exception</u>: the suffix <u>ed</u> makes a <u>one</u> syllable word after every consonant except <u>t</u> and <u>d</u>.

    <u>mix</u>ed   helped   smelled   lacked   cashed

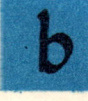

PRACTICE WORDS FOR SYLLABICATION

Rule #1	#2	#3	#4	#4 Exc.	Mixed
made	inside	unsafe	rested	smelled	bumper
film	leapfrog	depart	landed	scrubbed	railroad
street	popcorn	exchange	loudest	slipped	displease
bounce	lifeboat	uncut	softly	timed	printed
queer	carfare	dislike	painter	scared	seeded
clap	bookcase	reward	hardness	flashed	stinging
spring	snowman	mislay	matching	stripped	fixes
ground	sometime	adjust	safely	clicked	floats
jumps	rainbow	prepare	boxes	seemed	unlock

RULES FOR SYLLABICATION, CONTINUED

5. If there is <u>one</u> consonant between <u>two</u> vowels, the word is usually divided **after** the <u>consonant</u> if the first vowel sound is short. It is called a <u>closed</u> syllable.

    rob-in   com-ics   grav-el   pol-ish

6. If there is <u>one</u> consonant between <u>two</u> vowels, the word is usually divided after the first <u>vowel</u> if the vowel sound is long. It is called an <u>open syllable</u>.

    la-bor   mu-sic   pho-to   Po-lish

7. If <u>two</u> or more consonants come between <u>two</u> vowels, the word is usually divided between the <u>first</u> two consonants.

    let-ter   cof-fee   splen-did   hun-gry

<u>Exceptions</u>: blends and strong digraphs are not <u>separated</u>. The strong consonant digraphs are <u>sh</u>, <u>ch</u>, <u>ck</u>, <u>wh</u>, <u>th</u>.

    se-cret   gath-er   punch-es   pro-gram

rob ~ ~ ~ ~ in

PRACTICE WORDS FOR SYLLABICATION

Rule #5	#5	#6	#6	#7	#7 Exc.
punish	river	pilot	vocal	bottom	bother
chapel	promise	David	Friday	silver	breather
never	melon	stupid	pupil	chapter	stitches
tonic	clever	motel	locate	harbor	checking
second	model	frozen	tulip	basket	decree
magic	shadow	cozy	below	marvel	freshen
finish	medal	pony	label	number	cracker
phonics	senate	student	moment	yellow	flashing
seventh	novel	paper	holy	angry	cypress

 la-ter

RULES FOR SYLLABICATION, CONTINUED

8. If a vowel is sounded alone in a word, it makes a syllable by itself.

    a-go   o-bey   mon-u-ment   pi-a-no   vi-o-let

9. If two vowels are together in a word but are sounded separately, the word is divided between the two vowels.

    di-et   fu-el   ra-di-o   cre-ate

10. If a word ends in <u>le</u> <u>preceded</u> <u>by</u> <u>a</u> <u>consonant</u>, the word is usually divided before the consonant.

    tum-ble   twin-kle   tin-gle   ri-fle

<u>Exception:</u> The strong digraph <u>ck</u> is never divided.

    tack-le   trick-le   knuck-le

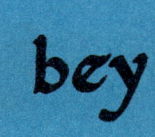

PRACTICE WORDS FOR SYLLABICATION

Rule #8	#8	#9	#10	#10 Exc.
about	imitate	polio	puddle	pickle
echo	litany	idea	wiggle	cackle
Irish	decorate	Iowa	jumble	shackle
idol	gasoline	period	fondle	chuckle
omit	uniform	denial	single	speckle
ivy	disagree	poem	bundle	cockle
item	kilowatt	museum	table	buckle
lily	eternal	oasis	cradle	tickle
unit	nominate	neon	needle	crackle

o - - - mit

Here's a "chal lenge" for you!

1

as tro naut
val en tine
con se quent
ad ver tise
in stru ment
re fresh ments
u ni ted
com mo tion
ex cite ment
sup ple ment
so lu tion

2

ad dress o graph
mis in ter pret
com bin a tion
em bar rass ment
can cel la tion
mon op o lize
con ver sa tion
as ton ish ment
ar tic u late
dis ap point ment
pan o ram ic

3

to tal i tar i an
ac cel er a tor
re vers i ble ness
e man ci pa tion
con sti tu tion al
mis ap pro pri ate
ap pre ci a tion
di ag nos ti cian
mis cel la ne ous
ter mi nol o gy
su per in tend ent

Are you ready for another challenge?

1	2	3
important	adventurous	abnormality
undisturbed	information	communication
requirements	executive	obligatory
occasion	conversation	laboratory
sympathize	subcommittee	disconformity
employment	prehistoric	appendicitis
nominate	anesthetic	approximation
insincere	memorandum	premeditated
dynamic	chrysanthemum	extemporaneous
microphone	transparently	configurationism
decipher	phosphorescence	overcapitalize

OUTLINE OF TERMINOLOGY FOR PHONETIC ELEMENTS

I. <u>Consonants</u>:

   A. <u>Single consonants</u>:

      All of the alphabet except a, e, i, o, u

   B. <u>Consonant digraphs</u>: a single consonant sound with double spelling

     1. <u>Basic digraphs</u>:

       ch, sh, wh, th, ~~th,~~ ng, nk, (zh)

     2. <u>Other digraphs</u>:

       ck, ph, gh, wr, kn, gn, mn, mb

   C. <u>Blends</u>:

      br, cr, dr, fr, gr, pr, tr, scr, str, bl, cl, fl, gl, pl, sc, sk, sm, sn, sp, st, sw, tw

II. <u>Vowels</u>:

   A. <u>Single vowels</u>:

      a, e, i, o, u and sometimes y and w (by and low)

   B. <u>Vowel digraphs</u>: a single vowel sound with double spelling

     1. <u>Regular digraphs</u>: the first vowel is always long, the second silent

       ai, ay, ea, ee, ei, ie, oa,

       oe, oo, ou, ow, ue, ui

OUTLINE OF TERMINOLOGY FOR PHONETIC ELEMENTS

B. <u>Digraphs,</u> continued

    2. <u>Irregular digraphs</u> - the first vowel is not long:

        a. First vowel is heard but it is not the long sound:

haul	(a_3)	head	($\breve{e}$)	too	(o_3)
lawn	(a_3)	cough	($\breve{o}$)	soup	(o_3)

        b. Second vowel is heard:

steak	($\bar{a}$)	shield	($\bar{e}$)	few	($\bar{u}$)
rough	($\breve{u}$)	could	(u_3)		

        c. Neither vowel is heard:

veil	($\bar{a}$)	true	(o_3)	earn	($u\underset{\smile}{r}$)
they	($\bar{a}$)	flew	(o_3)	took	(u_3)

C. <u>Diphthongs</u> - a double vowel sound with double spelling: vowel blends

    1. <u>Plain:</u> ou, ow, oi, oy

    2. <u>Murmur:</u> ar, or, er, ir, ur

N.B.   The third sound of a is the Italian a or $\ddot{a}$.
          The third sound of o is the same as Webster's long double o ($\overline{oo}$)
            and Thorndike's double dot $\ddot{u}$.
          The third sound of u is the same as Webster's short double o ($\breve{oo}$)
            and Thorndike's one dot $\dot{u}$.

The Alphabet

a b c d e f g h i j
k l m n o p q r s t
   u v w x y z

A B C D E F G H I J
K L M N O P Q R S T
   U V W X Y Z

DEFINITIONS

Phonics — the system of representing word sounds with letters.

Vowel — the alphabet letters a, e, i, o, u and sometimes y and w.

Syllable — a word or part of a word that contains one vowel sound.

Blend — two or three consonants said together, each keeping its own sound.

Diphthong — two vowels joined in one syllable to make a double sound. There are plain and murmur diphthongs.

Consonant digraph -- two consonants which together make one consonant sound

Vowel digraph — two vowels which together make one vowel sound.

Regular vowel digraph — the first vowel is long and the second is silent.

Irregular vowel digraph — can be any of the basic vowel sounds other than the long sound of the first vowel.

Schwa — the unstressed vowel sound which is pronounced like short u.

TABLE OF CONTENTS

PART ONE   Page

Short Vowels	8
Blends	28
Consonant Digraphs	31
Long Vowels	39
Magic e	41
Regular Vowel Digraphs	43
Consonant Digraphs	44
Blends	48
Third Sound of a, o, and u	53
Diphthongs	
Plain	55
Murmur	56
Suffix Rules	60
Consonant Rules for s, c, and g	65
Irregular Vowel Digraphs	70
ie	71
oo	72
ea	73
ew	75
ei	76
ou	77

TABLE OF CONTENTS

PART TWO   Page

Schwa --   81

Prefixes and Suffixes ------------------------------   82

Silent Letters --   84

Exceptions to Murmur Diphthongs --------------   86

Non-phonetic Words ------------------------------   88

Special Consonant Digraphs ---------------------   91

Three sounds for x - zh --------------------------   94

All the Consonant Rules -------------------------   95

All the Vowel Rules ------------------------------   96

Rules for Syllabication --------------------------   98

Outline of Terminology -------------------------- 106

Definitions -- 109